Peculiar Phenomenal Year 6 Poems

AF624541

Cassandra Polden

BookLeaf Publishing

Presentation by *BookLeaf Publishing*

Web: www.bookleafpub.com

E-mail: info@bookleafpub.com

ISBN: 9789357212243

First edition 2023

DEDICATION

This book is dedicated to many people but mainly to our beautiful teacher Miss Polden for helping us create our best work.

PREFACE

For weeks now they have been shown the ropes
submitting their pieces for publication with high hopes
21 poems in 21 days
creativity afforded a space to play
together these poems will be forever bound
per #TheWriteAngle Challenge on Amazon to be found
with tears in her eyes their fair teacher did share
for their determination, pride and courage she did care

- Cassandra Polden

The Post Office

A big red box full of mysteries
full of someone's written histories
a pile of letters and cards
travels away many yards
to people who are far away
delivering your messages on their way
whether rain or sun
the moment you see it is incredibly fun
fancy letter arriving at your door
the more you will see the more you will want
more
many people scattered around the globe
the number of letters could fill a wardrobe
but they serve with pride
one step then a long stride
bringing letters in the holidays
they run around in an endless maze
the only way they sleep at night
is when they have accomplished their letter
flight

- Zoe S

Umbrella

She is as black as the midnight sky
she is a protector, a living shelter for thee
her steel spine is as glossy as a timid river
reflecting on everyone who goes by
the tip of her head points up to the sky
guiding and aligning the stars as they smile
down on you
she wraps her arms around you as comfy and
cozy as a blanket

- Ella F

Music

It can be as loud as a thunderclap
or as soft as a cloud
old as a fossil
but futuristic too
glamourous as the Opera House
and as casual as the street
diverse as the many nations;
music

- Ryo G

Hello

Hello from the world below
I am someone you don’t know
you can’t tell me to go
I’ll always be in the world below
that slight glow
a few years ago
that was my hello
but now I am gone just so you know
as dark as a crow
as lonely as a single toe
that was me; your HELLO

- Alice M

The Tiger

He is the king of the jungle
that is as sly as a fox

he is a hungry beast
that is as fast as a cheetah

he is as soft as a kitten but
as fierce as a lion

he is your worst nightmare;
the tiger

- Ned T & Griff E

F22 Raptor

It is as deadly as a dinosaur
as cool as an iceberg
it is as stealthy as a cat
as quiet as a thief
it is as dangerous as a murderer
as technologically advanced as an atmospheric
scoop
it is as quick as a moon rocket
and so agile that it can out perform any other
aircraft
enemies fear seeing it in the sky
the raptor shoots them down like flies
equipped with Amraams and Sidewinder
missiles
nothing can match its superb aerial combat skills
built by Boeing and Lockheed Martin
the USA didn't let any other air forces have it
because they feared having it as a foe
loaded with missiles and ammunition
an amazing sight in the sky
with the black paint silhouetted against the blue
sky
flying by so quickly you don't even see it
the most advanced fighter in the skies
hugely expensive

claimed to be the best fighter ever
combining stealth technology with fighter,
ground-attack
and even electronic warfare capabilities
it is amazing and superb, the
F22 Raptor

- Nicolas C

The Moon

It influences us like a religion
it is the colour of a pigeon
people used to think it was made of cheese
they also thought it was covered by seas
it orbits the earth
it is death and birth
it can make us mad
or sad
a big, big rock floating in space
it played a big role in the space race
first to reach it was Apollo 11
it led to a massive “moon obsession”
we’ve driven on it with a rover
but before Apollo 17 it was over

- Marco H

Nature

Trees are swaying
while flowers are dancing
to the singing of the wind
the mountains go higher than clouds
while rocks are like broken down cars
the dirt is as grainy as rice
under the grass, pointy as a knife
the leaves are waving as they say hello
to the snow as white as dove feathers
the mirror water is as wild as a tiger
the sea blue sky contains
the clouds as fluffy as alpacas

this is nature

- Sashko B & Moritz B

Bunny

There once was a very cute bunny
who lived in a hole with his mummy
across the field he would hop
all the way home he would plop
where grass will fill up his tummy

he is as cute as clouds, as soft as marshmallow
he is a cushion that sits on your lounge
he is as white as snow, as cute as a button
he is a pogo-stick as he jumps though the
meadows

- Davey A

Different

You feel different and then sad
think you are sick and bad
you destroy everything
and you can only bring
sadness to the people here
your name sounds bad in every ear
you think you destroy what people love
destroy their hearts in a glove
so they will never love again
women will never have a man

but you don’t know what I think
cause I know there is a link
where everybody feels good
a place in the middle of a wood
so, remember when you feel different
it’s the unique people who change the world

\- Pia S

Friendship

An unbreakable bond
we're both quite fond
all the secrets we can’t bear
that we share
you make me feel free
with just us three
you pick me up when I'm down
turn that frown upside down
always honest
quite modest
that’s why I thank you
thank you for being you
for letting our bond be strong
for helping me find where I belong
we go through it all together;
together forever

- Chloe E

Ocean

It covers up sand
it is as big as Mars
it is as beautiful as a rainbow
when the sun goes down
this is the beautiful ocean

- Chloe S

The Llama

He is the living definition of cute
grazing peacefully on the green fields
he is large,
but inside he is as soft as marshmallow
his fur as soft and white as snow
he is the guardian of grass and the field
as strong as an elephant yet as gentle as a mouse
he troughs and ploughs through the field
scanning for pests
he is the custodian of the field;
he is Llama!

- Ted C

Be Different

You can be the only bird between clouds
the only dollar between pounds
don’t hide behind pounds or sit behind a tree
just be yourself and be free

- Carla A

The City of Wonder

A peaceful city at the edge of the ocean
a city full of wonder and commotion
no one knows where or how but the city of
Emton lays myth
it is to say on moonlit summers night
the city of Emton arises from the ground
one breezy summer's night one lucky child will
look out the window to see the beauty of Emton
16 seconds on the dot will the child be able to
look
once the child looks out the next night the lights
will be out
the child will be reborn that same night as an
Emon
and live on in the dreamland

- Emma S

Dogs

They are a human's best friend
support you through hard & good times
they will never leave your side
might know you your whole life
they will honour you until they are gone
will stand loyal to their owners

- Matthias C

My puppy dog is as smart as Calibri
as hungry as a bear
as curious as a koala
as annoying as a fly
chews on stuff like a beaver
but he is only 4 months old

- Frederik L

Here to Hear

What is an aeroplane without a single gear
for what do you need a spear
ears they are here to hear
lions you shouldn't get near
a murderer; oh dear!
It's healthy to eat a pear
unhealthy beer
it saves your life; fear
a steering wheel is to steer
some seas are crystal clear
is William Shakespeare
a good poet?

- Lucas L

Guess the Animal Haiku

Chicks are very cute
chickens for everyone here
they lay lots of eggs

They are small and grey
they go squeak and are quiet
cats hunt them a lot

Kittens are nice pets
cats are the best pets on earth
a small cat species

- Markus K

Mother Nature

It can be as loud as a thunderclap
or as quiet as a whisper
it can be as hectic as Nina and Sasha combined
or as calm as a meadow
it can be as harmful as a fight
or as harmless as a baby;
mother nature

- Amelie W

Pain

The pain of existence, the pain of life
the feeling that one day you're going to die
the feeling of sadness through your veins
trying to push away the aching pains

like a knife stabbing your heart
a wound that cuts so deep you fall apart
no one to talk to when you need a hand
no one to rely on when nothing goes to plan

you're too stressed to focus well
bad grades, bad relationships, you're locked in a cell
you're either too busy or have nothing to do
sometimes it's difficult to think you'll push through

slowly but surely that wound in your heart
will begin to heal and you'll stop falling apart
you still break and you fake that you're okay
but this time you're stronger and you'll make it through the day

- Sasha I & Nina O

Pixels

They are on the screen
yearning to be seen
upon rows and rows on your screen
making pictures and mixtures of colour
and digital fixtures

- Oskar B

www.ingramcontent.com/pod-product-compliance
Lightning Source LLC
Chambersburg PA
CBHW051718130826
49812CB00034B/1239
* 9 7 8 9 3 5 7 2 1 2 2 4 3 *